Crock Pot Cookbook for Smart People

Easy And Flavourful Recipes For People On A Budget. Regain Confidence And Improve Your Metabolism With Simple And Creative Recipes

Clara Smith

© Copyright 2021 - All rights reserved.

Table of Contents

Introduction

The crockpot has long been a favorite kitchen implement for the 'set-it-and-forget-it' meal. It's a wonderful invention by whoever thought it up, and it has saved many a few dollars on electricity by not needing to keep the stove and oven on for extended hours and all day. So, what really is a crockpot?

A crockpot is also called a slow cooker or a casserole crockpot. These nicknames refer to the same kitchen appliance, and it is one of the most used reheating methods today. It is basically a cooker with a glazed ceramic bowl that has a tight sealing lid. It is because of the liquid that will go in with the food. The crockpot is then plugged into an electrical socket in the kitchen for it to work.

The crockpot slow cooking method involves basically depositing the ingredients you desire to cook into the crockpot bowl (usually by stirring it with a wooden spoon or a ladle), adding the liquid of choice, cooking it for a few hours until it's done. These used to be the standard cooking methods in kitchens, and they have stayed the same with the invention of the crockpot. Nowadays, most crockpots have interiors thermostatically controlled to ensure that it's set at the right temperature during the cooking process to not over-cook your meals.

The best in crockpot slow cooking is finding that low and slow recipe. Recipes that are low in time length are usually very low in steps, and not much work is involved. It usually leads to the much sought after 'set it and forget it' kind of meal. Imagine not having to watch your meals cook slowly as you work on other tasks; you can avoid the temptation of peeking or checking on it too often and not having to worry about burning or crusting on the sides of your crockpot. When cooking at low heat, you don't have to worry about your meal exploding all over the kitchen or all the grease falling out and sticking to the bottom of your crock.

The best use of crockpot slow cooking is the convenience of the food, especially during holidays and parties. You can set the crockpot down on the table, and everyone can serve themselves. It is an excellent and great way to spend time with your guests and treat them well. There is nothing cheesier than eating the same dish fondue style. You get to enjoy slow cooking hotdogs for hours and hours without little ones surreptitiously taking off the top and poaching them in the pool of oil sitting beside the dish.

A crockpot is a very good way to use leftovers for a delicious meal. If you cook a large meal regularly and you have leftovers, put them in a crockpot with a liquid and let it cook. It will double the amount of food leftover or fed to the cat at the end of the week.

Crockpot cooking generally saves time, but it is also a low-budget way to cook. Slow cooking food can save you money because they are usually very low and easy to make. In fact, it is even possible to cook a meal with the last few pennies in your wallet. If you're on a tight budget and you don't have much to spend on your meals, the crockpot is the way to go.

Crockpots even make for a great gift since it's made in many shapes and sizes, from the really small, 1-quart crockpot to the huge 8 quarts or more. Any shape or size would be a welcome gift for anyone because everyone eats. Any occasion could be a good time to give someone a crockpot, and the more occasions you can name, the more crockpots you could make as gifts.

CHAPTER 1:

Breakfast

1.   Pumpkin-Nutmeg Pudding

Preparation Time: 15 Minutes Cooking Time: 6 to 7 Hours

Servings: 8

Ingredients:

- ¼ Cup melted butter, divided

- 2½ cups canned pumpkin purée

- 2 cups coconut milk

- 4 eggs 1 tablespoon pure vanilla extract

- 1 cup almond flour

- ½ cup granulated erythritol

- 2 ounces protein powder

- 1 teaspoon baking powder

- 1 teaspoon ground cinnamon

- ¼ teaspoon ground nutmeg

- Pinch ground cloves

Directions:

1. Grease the insert of the crockpot with 1 tablespoon of the butter. In a large bowl, whisk together the remaining butter, pumpkin, coconut milk, eggs, and vanilla until well blended.

2. In a small bowl, stir together the almond flour, erythritol, protein powder, baking powder, cinnamon, nutmeg, and cloves.

3. Add the dry fixings to the wet fixings and stir to combine. Pour the mixture into the insert. Cover then cook on low for 6 to 7 hours. Serve warm.

Nutrition: Calories: 265 Fat: 22g Protein: 13g Carbs: 8g

2.   **Buttery Coconut Bread**

Preparation Time: 10 Minutes

Cooking Time: 3 to 4 Hours

Servings: 8

Ingredients:

- 1 tablespoon butter, softened

- 6 large eggs

- ½ cup coconut oil, melted

- 1 teaspoon pure vanilla extract

- ¼ teaspoon liquid stevia

- 1 cup almond flour

- ½ cup coconut flour

- 1-ounce protein powder

- 1 teaspoon baking powder

Directions:

1. Grease an 8-by-4-inch loaf pan with the butter. In a medium bowl, whisk the eggs, oil, vanilla, and stevia until well blended.

2. In a small bowl, stir together the almond flour, coconut flour, protein powder, and baking powder until mixed. Add the dry fixings to the wet fixings and stir to combine.

3. Spoon the batter into the loaf pan then place the loaf pan on a rack in the crockpot. Cover then cook on low for 3 to 4 hours, until a knife inserted in the center comes out clean.

4. Cool the bread in the loaf pan for 15 minutes. Then take away the bread from the pan and place onto a wire rack to cool completely. Store in a sealed container in the refrigerator for up to 1 week.

Nutrition:

Calories: 336

Fat: 28g

Protein: 15g Carbs: 9g

3.   **Breakfast Sausage**

Preparation Time: 10 Minutes

Cooking Time: 3 Hours

Servings: 8

Ingredients:

- 1 tablespoon extra-virgin olive oil

- 2 pounds ground pork

- 2 eggs

- 1 sweet onion, chopped

- ½ cup almond flour

- 2 teaspoons minced garlic

- 2 teaspoons dried oregano

- 1 teaspoon dried thyme

- 1 teaspoon fennel seeds

- 1 teaspoon freshly ground black pepper

- ½ teaspoon salt

Directions:

1. Grease the insert of the crockpot with the olive oil. In a large bowl, stir together the pork, eggs, onion, almond flour, garlic, oregano, thyme, fennel seeds, pepper, and salt until well mixed.

2. Transfer the meat mixture to the crockpot's insert and shape it into a loaf, leaving about ½ inch between the sides and meat.

3. Cover, and if your crockpot has a temperature probe, insert it. Cook on low until it reaches an internal temperature of 150°F, about 3 hours. Slice in any way you prefer and serve.

Nutrition:

Calories: 341

Fat: 27g

Protein: 21g

Carbs: 1g

4.   Huevos Rancheros

Preparation Time: 10 Minutes

Cooking Time: 3 Hours

Servings: 8

Ingredients:

- 1 tablespoon extra-virgin olive oil

- 10 eggs

- 1 cup heavy (whipping) cream

- 1 cup shredded Monterey jack cheese, divided

- 1 cup prepared or homemade salsa

- 1 scallion, green and white parts, chopped

- 1 jalapeño pepper, chopped

- ½ teaspoon chili powder

- ½ teaspoon salt

- 1 avocado, chopped, for garnish

- 1 tablespoon chopped cilantro, for garnish

Directions:

1. Grease the crockpot with the olive oil. In a large bowl, whisk the eggs, heavy cream, ½ cup of the cheese, salsa, scallion, jalapeño, chili powder, and salt.

2. Pour the mixture into the insert and sprinkle the top with the remaining ½ cup of cheese. Cover then cook until the eggs are firm, about 3 hours on low.

3. Let the eggs cool slightly, then cut into wedges and serve garnished with avocado and cilantro.

Nutrition:

Calories: 302

Fat: 26g

Protein: 13g

Carbs: 5g

5.   Mediterranean Eggs

Preparation Time: 10 Minutes

Cooking Time: 5 to 6 Hours

Servings: 4

Ingredients:

- 1 tablespoon extra-virgin olive oil

- 12 eggs

- ½ cup coconut milk

- ½ teaspoon dried oregano

- ½ teaspoon freshly ground black pepper

- ¼ teaspoon salt

- 2 cups chopped spinach

- 1 tomato, chopped

- ¼ cup chopped sweet onion

- 1 teaspoon minced garlic

- ½ cup crumbled goat cheese

Directions:

1. Grease the crockpot with the olive oil. In a large bowl, whisk the eggs, coconut milk, oregano, pepper, and salt, until well blended.

2. Add the spinach, tomato, onion, and garlic, and stir to combine. Pour the egg mixture into the insert and top with the crumbled goat cheese. Cover then cook on low 5 to 6 hours, until it is set like a quiche. Serve warm.

Nutrition:

Calories: 349

Fat: 27g

Protein: 23g

Carbs: 5g

CHAPTER 2:

Mains

6.   Crock Pot Whole Chicken

Preparation time: 15 minutes

Cooking time: 5 hours

Servings: 10

Ingredients:

- 1 (5 lb.) chicken, with giblets removed

- 1 tablespoon sea salt

- ½ teaspoon paprika

- Black pepper to taste

- 8 ounces of baby carrots, chopped

- 4 large red potatoes, halved

- 1 yellow onion, peeled, quartered

- 1 Anaheim pepper, halved seeded

- 8 garlic cloves, peeled, smashed

- Handful of Italian parsley

Directions:

1. Rinse the chicken and pat dry. Mix salt and paprika together and season chicken with this along with black pepper. Scatter veggies on bottom of Crock Pot, place chicken on top of veggies.

2. Cook on high for 5 hours. Remove chicken from pot and allow to rest for about 10-minutes. Cut into pieces and serve.

Nutrition:

Calories: 289

Fat: 4.5 g

Carbs: 17 g Protein: 43.1 g

7.   Jalapeno Chicken Chili

Preparation time: 15 minutes Cooking time: 8 hours

Servings: 8

Ingredients:

- 1 medium onion, diced

- 3 garlic cloves, minced

- 1 red bell pepper, diced

- 2 jalapenos, seeds removed

- 1 (14-ounces) large sweet potato

- 1 lb. lean ground chicken

- 1 lb. lean ground beef

- 2 teaspoons smoked paprika

- 2 teaspoons chili powder

- 2 teaspoons dried oregano

- 2 teaspoons sea salt

- 1 teaspoon ground cumin

- ¼ teaspoon red pepper flakes

- 1 (14-ounce) can petite diced tomatoes

- Chopped scallions for garnish

- 8 ounces of avocado, diced

- 4 ounces goat cheese

Directions:

1. Place all the ingredients into your Crock Pot, except for goat cheese, scallions, and avocado. Cover and cook on LOW for 8 hours.

2. When done, break up meat using wooden spoon, then add in half of goat cheese. Serve garnished with scallions, avocado and remaining goat cheese.

Nutrition:

Calories: 285 Fat: 12 g Carbs: 20 g Protein: 25 g

8. Crustless Pizza

Preparation time: 15 minutes

Cooking time: 4 hours

Servings: 10

Ingredients:

- 2 lbs. ground beef

- Dried minced onion, garlic salt and pepper to taste

- 14-ounce jar pizza sauce

- 2 cups mozzarella cheese, shredded

- 2 cups pizza blend cheese, shredded

- Favorite pizza toppings

Directions:

1. In a skillet over medium-high heat brown your meat and drain.
    Put the beef and mozzarella cheese in a mixing bowl and mix
    together.

2. Spray your crock pot lightly with cooking spray. Spread beef mixture evenly on bottom of Crock Pot. Pour pizza sauce across the top and spread it out evenly.

3. Top with your pizza blend cheese and toppings. Cover and cook on low for 4 hours.

Nutrition:

Calories: 237

Fat: 25 g

Carbs: 7 g

Protein: 70 g

9. Roast Beef

Preparation time: 15 minutes

Cooking time: 8 hours

Servings: 6

Ingredients:

Seasoning Rub:

- 1 teaspoon garlic powder

- ¼ teaspoon rosemary

- 1 ½ teaspoons salt

- ¼ teaspoon thyme

- ¼ teaspoon oregano

- ¼ teaspoon basil

- ¼ teaspoon parsley

Main Ingredients:

- 2 1/2 lbs. boneless chuck roast

- 2 tablespoons olive oil

- 2 strips bacon

- 1 cup water or beef broth

- ¼ cup apple cider vinegar

- 2 tablespoons tomato paste

- ¾ teaspoon salt

- 4 stalks celery, chopped

- 1 small onion, chopped

- 2 garlic cloves, minced

- 2 bay leaves

- ½ cup of cauliflower florets, chopped small

Directions:

1. Combine seasonings and rub over the roast beef. Heat olive oil in large pan over medium-high heat and brown roast on all sides. Place roast into Crock Pot and cover with bacon strips.

2. Add water, tomato paste, vinegar, and salt into pan roast cooked in. Whisk to loosen up browned pieces from pan. Add onion, celery, garlic and bay leaves into Crock Pot.

3. Cook roast on low for 8 hours. Add in cauliflower during the last 30 minutes of cook time.

Nutrition:

Calories: 499

Fat: 23.1 g

Carbohydrates: 3.4 g

Protein: 65.3 g

CHAPTER 3:

Sides

10.   Cheesy Spaghetti Squash

Preparation Time: 25 minutes

Cooking time: 4 hours

Servings: 2

Ingredients:

- 10 oz spaghetti squash, peeled and seeded

- 1 tablespoon butter

- ½ teaspoon thyme

- 1 teaspoon paprika

- 1/3 cup water

- 2 oz Parmesan, sliced

Directions:

1. Grate the spaghetti squash and place it in the crockpot. Add the butter, thyme, paprika, and water. Stir the mixture gently with a spoon.

2. Then cover the squash with the sliced cheese and close the lid. Cook the meal for 4 hours on Low. Let the cooked squash rest for 15 minutes. Serve it!

Nutrition:

Calories 190

Fat 12.8g

Carbs 11.6g

Protein 10.3g

11.   Pesto Spaghetti Squash

Preparation Time: 15 minutes

Cooking time: 6 hours

Servings: 4

Ingredients:

- 1 cup spinach

- 2 tablespoons olive oil

- 1 oz pumpkin seeds, crushed

- 1-pound spaghetti squash

- 1 teaspoon butter

- ¾ cup water

Directions:

1. Chop the spaghetti squash and put it in the crockpot. Add butter and water. Close the lid and cook for 6 hours on Low.

2. Meanwhile, chop the spinach and place it in the blender. Add olive oil and pumpkin seeds. Blend the mixture until smooth.

3. When the spaghetti squash is cooked, transfer it into the serving

    bowls and sprinkle with the spinach (pesto) mixture. Serve it!

Nutrition:

Calories 144

Fat 11.9g

Carbs 9.4g

Protein 2.7g

12.   Zucchini Slices with Mozzarella

Preparation Time: 15 minutes

Cooking time: 1 hour

Servings: 4

Ingredients:

- 3 oz Mozzarella, sliced

- 1 zucchini, sliced

- 1 tablespoon olive oil

- 1 teaspoon butter

- 1 tablespoon coconut flakes, unsweetened

- 1 teaspoon minced garlic

Directions:

1. Sprinkle the zucchini slices with the olive oil, coconut flakes, and minced garlic. Place the zucchini slices in a flat layer on the bottom of the crockpot along with the butter.

2. Place a piece of mozzarella on top of each zucchini slice. Close the lid and cook the meal for 1 hour on High. Serve hot!

Nutrition:

Calories 112

Fat 8.7g

Carbs 2.8g

Protein 6.7g

13.   Kale Mash with Blue Cheese

Preparation Time: 15 minutes

Cooking time: 5 hours

Servings: 3

Ingredients:

- 3 oz Blue cheese

- 1 cup Italian dark-leaf kale

- ¾ cup almond milk, unsweetened

- 1 tablespoon butter

- 1 teaspoon salt

- 1 teaspoon ground black pepper

Directions:

1. Chop the kale and place it in the crockpot. Add almond milk, salt, and ground black pepper. Close the lid and cook the kale for 5 hours on Low.

2. Meanwhile, chop Blue cheese and butter. Combine the cooked kale with the butter and stir it until butter is melted. Add the Blue cheese and stir it gently. Serve!

Nutrition:

Calories 285

Fat 26.3g

Carbs 6.8g

Protein 8.2g

14.   Black Soybeans

Preparation Time: 10 minutes

Cooking time: 7 hours

Servings: 6

Ingredients:

- 10 oz black soybeans

- 2 cups water

- 1 teaspoon salt

- 1 teaspoon chili flakes

- 1 tablespoon dried dill

- 1 teaspoon butter

Directions:

1. Place the black soybeans, water, salt, and chili flakes in the crockpot. Close the lid and cook the soybeans for 7 hours on Low.

2. Place the cooked soybeans in the bowls and combine with butter. Stir and serve!

Nutrition:

Calories 218

Fat 10.1g

Carbs 14.6g

Protein 17.4g

CHAPTER 4:

Seafood

15. Calamari Curry

Preparation Time: 10 minutes

Cooking Time: 3 hours

Servings: 2

Ingredients:

- 1-pound calamari rings

- ½ tablespoon yellow curry paste

- 1 cup coconut milk

- ½ teaspoon turmeric powder

- ½ cup chicken stock

- 2 garlic cloves, minced

- ½ tablespoon coriander, chopped

- A pinch of salt and black pepper

- 2 tablespoons lemon juice

Directions:

1. In your crockpot, mix the rings with the curry paste, coconut milk and the other ingredients, toss, put the lid on and cook on High for 3 hours. Divide the curry into bowls and serve.

Nutrition:

Calories 200

Fat 12g

Carbs 6g

Protein 11g

16.   Balsamic Trout

Preparation Time: 10 minutes Cooking Time: 3 hours

Servings: 2 ngredients:

- 1-pound trout fillets, boneless

- ½ cup chicken stock

- 2 garlic cloves, minced

- 2 tablespoons balsamic vinegar

- ½ teaspoon cumin, ground

- Salt and black pepper to the taste

- 1 tablespoon parsley, chopped 1 tablespoon olive oil

Directions:

1. In your crockpot, mix the trout with the stock, garlic and the other ingredients, toss gently, put the lid on and cook on High for 3 hours. Divide the mix between plates and serve.

Nutrition: Calories 200 Fat 12g Carbs 6g Protein 9g

17.   Oregano Shrimp Bowls

Preparation Time: 10 minutes

Cooking Time: 1 hour

Servings: 2

Ingredients:

- 1-pound shrimp, peeled and deveined

- ½ cup cherry tomatoes, halved

- ½ cup baby spinach

- 1 tablespoon lime juice

- 1 tablespoon oregano, chopped

- ¼ cup fish stock

- ½ teaspoon sweet paprika

- 2 garlic cloves, chopped

- A pinch of salt and black pepper

Directions:

1. In your crockpot, mix the shrimp with the cherry tomatoes, spinach and the other ingredients, toss, put the lid on and cook on High for 1 hour. Divide everything between plates and serve.

Nutrition:

Calories 211

Fat 13g

Carbs 7g

Protein 11g

18.   Creamy Sea Bass

Preparation Time: 15 minutes Cooking time: 2 hours

Servings: 4

Ingredients:

- 1-pound sea bass fillets, boneless

- 1 teaspoon garlic powder

- ½ teaspoon Italian seasoning

- ½ teaspoon salt

- ¼ cup heavy cream

- 1 tablespoon butter

Directions:

1. In the crockpot, mix the sea bass with the other ingredients. Close the crockpot lid and cook for 2 hours on High.

Nutrition: Calories 231 Fat 14.9g arbs 7.4g Protein 24.2g

19.   Oregano Crab

Preparation Time: 10 minutes Cooking time: 40 minutes

Servings:

Ingredients:

- 1 tablespoon dried oregano

- 2 cups crab meat

- ½ cup spring onions, chopped

- ¾ teaspoon minced garlic

- 1 tablespoon lemon juice

- ½ cup of coconut milk

Directions:

1. In the crockpot, mix the crab with oregano and the other ingredients and close the lid. Cook for 40 minutes on High, divide into bowls, and serve.

Nutrition: Calories 151 Fat 3g Carbs 6g Protein 5g

CHAPTER 5:

Poultry

20.   Wine Chicken

Preparation time: 15 minutes

Cooking Time: 3 Hours

Servings: 4

Ingredients:

- 1 cup red wine

- 1-pound chicken breast, skinless, boneless, chopped

- 1 anise star

- 1 teaspoon cayenne pepper

- 2 garlic cloves, crushed

Directions:

1. Pour red wine in the Crock Pot. Add anise star, cayenne pepper, and garlic cloves. Then add chopped chicken and close the lid.

2. Cook the meal on High for 3 hours. Serve the chicken with hot wine sauce.

Nutrition:

Calories 182

Protein 24.2g

Carbohydrates 2.4g

Fat 2.9g

21.   **Chicken in Sweet Soy Sauce**

Cooking Time: 6 Hours

Servings: 6

Ingredients:

- ½ cup of soy sauce

- 2 teaspoons maple syrup

- ½ teaspoon ground cinnamon

- 6 chicken thighs, skinless, boneless

- ¼ cup of water

Directions:

1. Pour water and soy sauce in the Crock Pot. Add chicken thighs, ground cinnamon, and maple syrup. Close the lid and cook the meal on Low for 6 hours.

Nutrition: Calories 295 Protein 43.6g Carbohydrates 3.3g Fat 10.8g

22.   Chicken Florentine

Preparation time: 15 minutes

Cooking Time: 8 Hours

Servings: 4

Ingredients:

- 4 chicken breasts, bones and skin removed

- Salt and pepper to taste

- 2 cups parmesan cheese, divided

- ½ cup heavy cream

- 1 cup baby spinach, rinsed

Directions:

1. Place the chicken in the crockpot. Season with salt and pepper to taste. Stir in half of the parmesan cheese. Close the lid and cook on low for 8 hours or on high for 6 hours.

2. Halfway through the cooking time, pour in the heavy cream. Continue cooking. An hour after the cooking time, add in the baby spinach. Cook until the spinach has wilted.

Nutrition:

Calories: 553

Carbohydrates: 3g

Protein: 48g

Fat: 32g

23.   Lemony Chicken

Preparation time: 15 minutes Cooking Time: 4 Hours

Servings: 6 Ingredients:

- 1 whole chicken, cut into medium pieces

- Salt and black pepper to the taste

- Zest of 2 lemons

- Juice of 2 lemons

- Lemon rinds from 2 lemons

Directions:

1. Put chicken pieces in your Crock Pot, season with salt and pepper to the taste, drizzle lemon juice, add lemon zest and lemon rinds, cover and cook on High for 4 hours.

2. Discard lemon rinds, divide chicken between plates, drizzle sauce from the Crock Pot over it and serve.

Nutrition: Calories 334 Fat 24g Carbs 4.5g Protein 27g

24.   Chicken Stuffed with Plums

Preparation time: 15 minutes

Cooking Time: 4 Hours

Servings: 6

Ingredients:

- 6 chicken fillets

- 1 cup plums, pitted, sliced

- 1 cup of water

- 1 teaspoon salt

- 1 teaspoon white pepper

Directions:

1. Beat the chicken fillets gently and rub with salt and white pepper. Then put the sliced plums on the chicken fillets and roll them. Secure the chicken rolls with toothpicks and put in the Crock Pot.

2. Add water and close the lid. Cook the meal on High for 4 hours. Then remove the chicken from the Crock Pot, remove the toothpicks and transfer in the serving plates.

Nutrition:

Calories 283

Protein 42.4g

Carbohydrates 1.6g

Fat 10.9g

CHAPTER 6:

Meat

25. Beef Sauté with Endives

Preparation time: 10 minutes

Cooking time: 8 hours

Servings: 4

Ingredients:

- 1-pound beef sirloin, chopped

- 1 oz. endives, roughly chopped

- 1 teaspoon peppercorns

- 1 carrot, diced

- 1 onion, sliced

- 1 cup of water

- ½ cup tomato juice

Directions:

1. Mix beef with onion, carrot, and peppercorns. Place the mixture in the crockpot. Add water and tomato juice.

2. Then close the lid and cook it on High for 5 hours. After this, add endives and cook the meal for 3 hours on Low.

Nutrition:

Calories 238

Protein 35.4g

Carbohydrates 6.4g

Fat 7.2g

26. Sweet Beef

Preparation time: 10 minutes Cooking time: 5 hours

Servings: 4

Ingredients:

- 1-pound beef roast, sliced

- 1 tablespoon maple syrup

- 2 tablespoons lemon juice

- 1 teaspoon dried oregano

- 1 cup of water

Directions:

1. Mix water with maple syrup, lemon juice, and dried oregano. Then pour the liquid into the crockpot. Add beef roast and close the lid. Cook the meal on High for 5 hours.

Nutrition: Calories 227 Protein 34.5g Carbohydrates 3.8g Fat 7.2g

27.   Thyme Beef

Preparation time: 15 minutes Cooking time: 5 hours

Servings: 2

Ingredients:

- 1 pound beef sirloin, chopped

- 1 tablespoon dried thyme

- 1 tablespoon olive oil

- ½ cup of water 1 teaspoon salt

Directions:

1. Preheat the skillet well. Then mix beef with dried thyme and olive oil. Put the meat in the hot skillet and roast for 2 minutes per side on high heat.

2. Then transfer the meat to the crockpot. Add salt and water. Cook the meal on High for 5 hours.

Nutrition: Calories 274 Protein 34.5g Carbohydrates 0.9g Fat 14.2g

28.   Hot Beef

Preparation time: 15 minutes Cooking time: 8 hours

Servings: 4

Ingredients:

- 1-pound beef sirloin, chopped

- 2 tablespoons hot sauce

- 1 tablespoon olive oil

- ½ cup of water

Directions:

1. In the shallow bowl, mix hot sauce with olive oil. Then mix beef sirloin with hot sauce mixture and leave for 10 minutes to marinate.

2. Put the marinated beef in the crockpot. Add water and close the lid. Cook the meal on Low for 8 hours.

Nutrition: Calories 241 Protein 34.4g Carbohydrates 0.1g Fat 10.6g

29.   Beef Chops with Sprouts

Preparation time: 10 minutes

Cooking time: 7 hours

Servings: 5

Ingredients:

- 1-pound beef loin

- ½ cup bean sprouts

- 1 cup of water

- 1 tablespoon tomato paste

- 1 teaspoon chili powder

- 1 teaspoon salt

Directions:

1. Cut the beef loin into 5 beef chops and sprinkle the beef chops with chili powder and salt. Then place them in the crockpot.

2. Add water and tomato paste. Cook the meat on low for 7 hours. Then transfer the cooked beef chops onto the plates, sprinkle

with tomato gravy from the crockpot, and top with bean sprouts.

Nutrition:

Calories 175

Protein 5.2g

Carbohydrates 1.6g

Fat 7.8g

CHAPTER 7:

Vegetables

30.   Lemon Asparagus

Preparation time: 8 minutes

Cooking time: 5 hours

Servings: 2

Ingredients:

- 8 oz. asparagus

- ½ cup butter - juice of 1 lemon

- Zest of 1 lemon, grated

- ½ teaspoon turmeric

- 1 teaspoon rosemary, dried

Directions:

1. In your crockpot, mix the asparagus with butter, lemon juice and the other Ingredients: and close the lid. Cook the vegetables on Low for 5 hours. Divide between plates and serve.

Nutrition:

Calories: 60

Carbs: 4g

Fat: 5g

Protein: 2g

31.   Lime Green Beans

Preparation time: 10 minutes Cooking time: 2.5 hours

Servings: 5 Ingredients:

- 1-pound green beans, trimmed and halved

- 2 spring onions, chopped

- 2 tablespoons lime juice

- ½ teaspoon lime zest, grated

- 2 tablespoons olive oil

- ¼ teaspoon ground black pepper

- ¾ teaspoon salt - ¾ cup of water

Directions:

1. In the crockpot, mix the green beans with the spring onions and the other Ingredients: and close the lid. Cook for 2.5 hours on High.

Nutrition: Calories: 100 Carbs: 19g Fat: 0g Protein: 6g

32.   Cheese Asparagus

Preparation time: 10 minutes Cooking time: 3 hours

Servings: 4

Ingredients:

- 10 oz. asparagus, trimmed

- 4 oz. Cheddar cheese, sliced

- 1/3 cup butter, soft

- 1 teaspoon turmeric powder

- ½ teaspoon salt

- ¼ teaspoon white pepper

Directions:

1. In the crockpot, mix the asparagus with butter and the other Ingredients, put the lid on and cook for 3 hours on High.

Nutrition: Calories: 260 Carbs: 38g Fat: 7g Protein: 11g

33. Creamy Broccoli

Preparation time: 15 minutes Cooking time: 1 hour

Servings: 4 Ingredients:

- ½ cup coconut cream

- 2 cups broccoli florets

- 1 teaspoon mint, dried

- 1 teaspoon garam masala

- 1 teaspoon salt

- 1 tablespoon almonds flakes

- ½ teaspoon turmeric

Directions:

1. In the crockpot, mix the broccoli with the mint and the other Ingredients. Close the lid and cook vegetables for 1 hour on High. Divide between plates and serve.

Nutrition: Calories: 93 Carbs: 11g Fat: 5g Protein: 2g

CHAPTER 8:

Soups & Stews

34. Cauliflower Chicken Chili

Preparation time: 15 minutes Cooking time: 8 hours

Servings: 6

Ingredients:

Chili:

- 1/2 head diced cauliflower

- 1 diced onion 1 diced red pepper

- 1 diced poblano pepper

- 2 minced garlic cloves

- 1 28- oz. pack tomato puree organic

- ½ cup of chicken stock

- 2 tbsp chili powder

- ¼ - ½ tsp chipotle flakes chili

- 1 tsp sea salt

- ½ tsp freshly powdered pepper

- 6 large chunks skinless thighs of chicken

Toppings:

- 1 avocado 1 lime

- fresh cilantro

Directions:

1. Place the chili ingredients inside the crockpot and mix to combine. Cook using a low setting for 8 hours. Dice the lime, cilantro, and cube avocado. Add these according to your taste

Nutrition: Calories: 289 Fat: 10g Carbs: 24g Protein: 27g

35.   Low-Carb Oxtail Soup

Preparation time: 15 minutes

Cooking time: 4 hours

Servings: 8

Ingredients:

- 3 1/2 lb. oxtails

- ¼cup of ghee

- 1-2 sprigs thyme & rosemary

- 3 of bay leaves

- ¼ tsp minced cloves

- 2 tbsp lemon juice

- 2 - 2 ½liters water

- 1 medium diced rutabaga

- 1 large unsweetened tin tomato

- 2 cups chopped green beans

- 2 medium sliced leeks

- 2 medium sliced celery stalks,

- salt & pepper

Directions:

1. Turn the meat brown and add to crockpot and set on high temperature and cook for 4 hours. Place the vegetables, combine the rosemary, bay leaves, thyme, and cloves.

2. Add water and some lemon juice. Carry it to the boiling point and turn the heat down. Cover it and simmer and stop once the meat is tender and leaves the bones.

3. After approximately 3 hours, take meat from the pot using kitchen tongs. Allow oxtails to cool down and shred meat.

4. Ready the vegetables as the meat is cooling. Peel the rutabaga and dice into around 1-inch pieces. Transfer to the pot, place a lid and allow it to cook for around 10 minutes.

5. Place the tomatoes, sliced leeks, celery stalks, and green beans. Leave it on the heat for further 10-15 minutes. Place the

shredded meat inside and pour water if required. Season using salt and pepper.

Nutrition:

Calories: 371

Fat: 22g

Carbs: 7g

Protein: 32g

36.   Autumn Beef & Vegetable Stew

Preparation time: 15 minutes

Cooking time: 7 hours

Servings: 10

Ingredients:

- 3 lb. boneless beef steaks

- ½cup lard

- 1 white onion medium

- 4 cloves of garlic

- 1 large unsweetened chopped tomatoes tin

- 1 cup of broth

- 2 tbsp powdered cumin

- 1 tbsp of paprika

- 1 tsp minced ginger

- 1 tsp powdered chili

- 1 tsp powdered coriander seeds

- 1 tsp powdered turmeric

- 2 of bay leaves

- 2 of cinnamon sticks

- 1 ½ tsp of salt

- freshly powdered black pepper

- 1 medium rutabaga

- 4-5 medium marrow squash or zucchini

Directions:

1. Preheat crockpot to high temperature. Dry the braising steaks with a paper towel and season using salt and pepper.

2. Grease the pan using 1/4 cup of ghee and add three steaks at one instance. Transfer them to the preheated crockpot once they are lightly browned.

3. Dice and peel the garlic and the onion. Add to the pan and turn them brown. Place tomatoes, chili powder, paprika, ginger,

broth, turmeric, cumin, and ground coriander seeds. Mix it all and add to crockpot.

4. Place cinnamon sticks plus bay leaves. Place a lid over it and let it cook for 3 hours before rutabaga is added.

5. Cook for one more hour and dice the zucchini in the meantime. Then add zucchini and mix. Take the bay leaves, and cinnamon sticks out. Cook for 2 more hours.

Nutrition:

Calories: 533

Fat: 40g

Carbs: 8g

Protein: 31g

37. Chicken Pot Pie Soup

Preparation time: 15 minutes

Cooking time: 6 hours

Servings: 6

Ingredients:

- 1–1.5 lb. chicken breasts, boneless and skinless

- 2 tbsp of butter

- ½ cup of mixed veggies

- ¼ small diced onion

- ¼ tsp of pink salt

- ¼ tsp of pepper

- 2 minced garlic cloves

- 1 3/4 cups heavy cream

- 3 cups of chicken broth

- 1 oz of cream cheese

- 1 tsp of poultry seasoning

- ¼ tsp of rosemary

- pinch of thyme

- ½ tsp of Xanthan Gum

Directions:

1. Prepare 1½ pound chicken in the crockpot with spices. Add a cup of chicken broth and cook at high temperature for 3 hours.

2. Sautee onion, garlic cloves, pepper, mixed veggies, and salt in 2tbsp butter placed skillet. Insert the whipping cream, remaining chicken broth, and cream cheese in the crockpot.

3. Place a lid over it and on high-temperature cook for 45 minutes.

Nutrition:

Calories: 432

Fat: 35.g

Carbs: 3g

Protein: 20g

38. Jalapeno Popper Soup

Preparation time: 15 minutes

Cooking time: 6 hours

Servings: 8

Ingredients:

- 1 ½ lb. chicken breasts boneless skinless

- 3 tbsp butter

- 2 minced garlic cloves

- ½ chopped onion

- ½ chopped green pepper

- 2 chopped seeded jalapenos

- ½ lb. crumbled cooked bacon

- 6 oz softened cream cheese

- 3 cups of chicken broth

- ½ cup of heavy cream

- ¼ tsp of paprika

- 1 tsp cumin

- 1 tsp salt

- ½ tsp pepper

- ¾ cup of Monterrey Cheese

- ¾ cup of Cheddar Cheese

- ½ tsp of xanthan gum

Directions:

1. Add butter to the pan, then sauté onions, jalapenos, seasonings, and green peppers. Add mixture to the crockpot and place chicken breasts.

2. Cook for 6 hours on a low setting. Take chicken out and make bits of it and then add back. Add cream cheese, prepared bacon stirring, and whipping cream.

3. Cook for 10 more minutes. Sprinkle with xanthan gum and simmer for 15 minutes. Serve with cheddar cheese and bacon on top.

Nutrition:

Calories: 571

Fat: 40g

Carbs: 2g

Protein: 40g

CHAPTER 9:

Snacks

39.   Eggplant Rolls with Meat

Preparation time: 15 minutes

Cooking Time: 26 Hours

Servings: 6

Ingredients:

- 2 eggplants

- 5 oz chicken fillet

- 1 teaspoon salt

- 1 teaspoon ground black pepper

- 3 oz Mozzarella, sliced

- 2 tablespoons butter

Directions:

1. Slice the eggplant lengthwise. Mix the salt and ground black pepper. Chop the chicken fillet and sprinkle it with the spices.

2. Place a small amount of the meat mix on each of the eggplant slices. Roll the eggplant slices, enclosing the meat, and secure with a toothpick.

3. Place the eggplant rolls in the crockpot and add water and butter. Cook the rolls for 6 hours. Chill the eggplant rolls slightly. Serve!

Nutrition:

Calories 165

Fat 8.4g

Carbs 11.5g

Protein 12.7g

40. Cheesy Zucchini Crisps

Preparation time: 15 minutes Cooking Time: 2.5 Hours

Servings: 2

Ingredients:

- 2 oz zucchini, sliced

- 1 oz Parmesan, grated

- 1 teaspoon olive oil ½ teaspoon chili flakes

Directions:

1. Place the olive oil in the crockpot. Place the zucchini slices in the crockpot in one layer. Sprinkle the zucchini slices with chili flakes and grated Parmesan.

2. Close the lid and cook the zucchini for 2.5 hours on High. Serve the cooked snack immediately!

Nutrition:

Calories 70 Fat 5.4g Carbs 1.5g Protein 4.9g

41.   **Butter Pork Ribs**

Preparation time: 15 minutes Cooking Time: 7 Hours

Servings: 4

Ingredients:

- 10 oz pork ribs

- 3 tablespoons butter, soft

- 1/3 cup coconut cream

- 1 teaspoon turmeric powder

- ½ teaspoon salt

- 1 teaspoon garlic powder

Directions:

1. In the crockpot, mix the pork with soft butter and the other ingredients. Close the lid and cook the pork ribs for 7 hours on Low.

Nutrition: alories 321 Fat 14.8g Carbs 6.5g Protein 19.7g

42.   Bacon Wrapped Duck Roll

Preparation time: 15 minutes

Cooking Time: 3 Hours

Servings: 12

Ingredients:

- 1-pound duck breast

- 5 oz bacon, sliced

- 1 teaspoon salt

- ½ teaspoon ground black pepper

- 1 teaspoon butter

- 1 teaspoon cayenne pepper

- 4 tablespoons water

Directions:

1. Beat the duck breast gently to flatten. Sprinkle the duck breast with the salt, ground black pepper, and cayenne pepper. Spread the butter on the duck breast and roll it.

2. Wrap the duck breast in the bacon and put it in the crockpot. Add the water and cook the duck roll for 3 hours on High. When the duck roll is cooked, slice it and enjoy!

Nutrition:

Calories 116

Fat 6.8g

Carbs 0.3g

Protein 12.7g

43. Chestnut Cream

Preparation time: 15 minutes

Cooking Time: 3 Hours

Servings: 6

Ingredients:

- 11 oz. water

- 1 ½ lbs. chestnuts

Directions:

1. In your crockpot, mix sugar with water and chestnuts, stir, cover and cook on Low for 3 hours. Blend using your immersion blender, divide into small cups and serve. Enjoy!

Nutrition:

Calories: 102

Fat: 1 g

Carbs: 5 g

Protein: 3 g

CHAPTER 10:

Desserts

44.   Coffee Cake

Preparation time: 15 minutes

Cooking time: 2-3 hours

Servings: 10

Ingredients:

- ½ cup sour cream

- 1/3 cup coffee

- ½ cup softened butter

- 3 eggs

- ½ cup sugar substitute (Swerve)

- 2 ¼ cups almond flour

- 2 ½ tsp baking powder

Syrup:

- 1/3 cup Water

- 1/3 cup sweetener

- ½ tsp instant coffee

Directions:

1. Take a medium bowl, conjoin the sour cream, coffee, until smooth. Add softened butter, stir well. Mix everything until smooth. Add the eggs, whisk all the time. Stir the sweetener.

2. Take another bowl, conjoin baking powder and almond flour. Put this mixture into the coffee mix. After you have combined all the mixtures, pour this into the Crock Pot covered with cooking spray.

3. Cover and cook on low for 2-3 hours. Check with a toothpick if the cake is ready.

4. Prepare the syrup – mix the water and Swerve on a medium heat. Whisk until all the ingredients are dissolved. Pour the instant coffee. Let it cool a little.

5. Once the cake is ready, remove it to the plate, pour the syrup over it. Cut and enjoy!

Nutrition:

Calories: 286

Carbs: 47g

Fat: 9g

Protein: 4g

45.   **Angel Food Cake**

Preparation time: 15 minutes

Cooking time: 0 hours

Servings: 8

Ingredients:

- ¾ cup Sweetener

- ½ cup Almond flour

- ¼ tsp Kosher salt

- 5 large Egg whites

- ½ tsp Cream of tartar

- 1 tsp Vanilla extract

- Macerated Strawberries

- Whipped cream

- Strawberries for dressing

Directions:

1. Firmly wring a 3-foot length of foil (aluminum foil), after this shape it into a zigzag form width-wise the oval or round Crock Pot. Just try to create a rack, adding 1 cup of water.

2. Place the top of the Crock Pot and set on low after this. Take a medium bowl, whisk together flour, sweetener, salt and set aside everything.

3. Take another little bowl, crack the eggs (whites) and add slowly tartar. Using the blender or the food processor, mix everything on a medium speed. It takes usually 1-2 minutes. Add vanilla.

4. Pour the mixture with sweetener from the first bowl into the second one, whisk all together. Transfer the batter to a loaf pan and smooth top.

5. Place the loaf pan into the Crock Pot, press into the aluminum foil rack just to ensure the level of the pan. Take a clean kitchen towel and drape over the Crock Pot. Put the lead over it.

6. Put the Crock Pot on low approximately 2-3 hours. Once 1,5 hours is over start to check the readiness of the cake in the Crock Pot.

7. Once the cake is ready, remove the pan from the Crock Pot and let it cool about 20 minutes. Using a knife, run it around the edges separating the ready cake from the pan.

8. Remove it to the serving plate. Dress with macerated strawberries at will and the whipped cream. Bon Appetite!

Nutrition:

Calories: 140

Carbs: 32g

Fat: 0g

Protein: 3g

46. Poached Pears with Amaretto

Preparation time: 15 minutes

Cooking time: 4 hours

Servings: 6-8

Ingredients:

- ½ cup amaretto liqueur

- 1 cup pear nectar

- 1½ cups firmly packed light brown sugar

- ½ cup (1 stick) unsalted butter, melted

- 6 firm red pears, peeled and cored

- ½ cup crushed amaretti cookies (about 6)

- ½ cup chopped almonds, toasted

Directions:

1. Combine the amaretto, nectar, sugar, and butter in the crockpot and stir until the sugar is dissolved.

2. Stand the pears in the liquid, stem-ends up. Cover and cook on low for 4 hours until the pears are tender.

3. Combine the cookie crumbs and almonds in a small bowl and set aside. Uncover the pears and allow to cool. Serve each pear in sauce and sprinkled with almond mixture.

Nutrition:

Calories: 241

Carbs: 49g

Fat: 4g

Protein: 2g

47.   **Caramel Pear Cake**

Preparation time: 15 minutes

Cooking time: 2-3 hours

Servings: 6

Ingredients:

- 6 medium pears, peeled and sliced

- ¼ cup heavy whipping cream

- ¾ cup packed brown sugar

- 1 teaspoon cornstarch

- 1 tablespoon chopped crystallized ginger

- 2 teaspoons lemon juice

- ½ teaspoon ground cinnamon

- 2 tablespoons butter, melted

- Grilled pound cake, whipped topping and sliced almonds

Directions:

1. In the crockpot, combine all the ingredients except for the cake. Stir to mix well. Cover and cook on low for 2 to 3 hours or until heated through.

2. Serve warm over pound cake. Top with whipped topping, then sprinkle with almonds.

Nutrition:

Calories: 220

Carbs: 25g

Fat: 12g

Protein: 3g

48.   Lemony Pudding Cake

Preparation time: 15 minutes

Cooking time: 2-3 hours

Servings: 5-6

Ingredients:

- 3 eggs, whites and yolks separated

- 1 teaspoon lemon zest

- ¼ cup lemon juice

- 3 tablespoons butter, melted

- 1½ cups milk

- ¾ cup sugar

- ¼ cup flour

- 1/8 teaspoon salt

Directions:

1. Beat the eggs whites until stiff peaks form in a bowl. Set aside. Beat the eggs yolks in a separate bowl. Blend in the lemon zest, lemon juice, butter, and milk.

2. In a third bowl, combine the sugar, flour, and salt. Add to the egg-lemon mixture, beating until smooth.

3. Fold them into the beaten egg whites. Spoon the mixture into the crockpot. Cover and cook on high for 2 to 3 hours. Serve warm.

Nutrition:

Calories: 342

Carbs: 36g

Fat: 20g

Protein: 0g

49.   Apple Cake with Walnuts

Preparation time: 15 minutes

Cooking time: 4 hours

Servings: 8-10

Ingredients:

- 2 cups sugar

- 1 cup olive oil

- 2 eggs

- 1 teaspoon vanilla

- 2 cups chopped apples

- 2 cups flour

- 1 teaspoon salt

- 1 teaspoon baking soda

- 1 teaspoon nutmeg

- 1 cup chopped walnuts

Directions:

1. Beat together the sugar, oil, and eggs in a large bowl. Add vanilla and apples. Mix well. Sift together flour, salt, baking soda, and nutmeg in a bowl. Add dry ingredients and nuts to the apple mixture. Stir well.

2. Pour batter into greased and floured cake pan that fits into the crockpot. Cover with pan's lid, or greased foil. Place pan in the crockpot, then cover.

3. Bake on high for 3½ to 4 hours. Let cake stand in pan for 5 minutes after removing from the crockpot. Remove cake from pan, slice, and serve.

Nutrition:

Calories: 172

Carbs: 23g

Fat: 8g

Protein: 2g

50. Lush Fruity Cake

Preparation time: 15 minutes

Cooking time: 2-3 hours

Servings: 8-10

Ingredients:

- 1 (20-ounce / 567-g) can crushed pineapple

- 1 (21-ounce / 595-g) can blueberry or cherry pie filling

- 1 (18½-ounce / 524-g) package yellow cake mix

- Cinnamon, to taste

- ½ cup butter

- 1 cup chopped nuts

- Vanilla ice cream, for serving

- Cooking spray

Directions:

1. Spritz the crockpot with cooking spray. Spread layers of pineapple, blueberry pie filling, and dry cake mix. Be careful not to mix the layers. Sprinkle with cinnamon.

2. Top with thin layers of butter and nuts. Cover. Cook on high for 2 to 3 hours. Serve with vanilla ice cream.

Nutrition:

Calories: 120

Carbs: 28g

Fat: 1g

Protein: 0g

Conclusion

You have to the end of this amazing cookbook, but always remember that this is not the end of your cooking journey with the crockpot; but instead, this is your stepping stone towards more cooking glory. We hope you have found your favorite recipes that are time-saving and money-saving.

Now that you know how Crockpot works and the many benefits of using it, maybe it is time for you to buy one for your family, in case you haven't owned one. When it comes to time spent preparing meals for your family, Crock-Pot is a lifesaver. If you are a busy person, a powerful solution is to use the crockpot.

You will also love to own one if you want to make your life simpler at work if you want to make your life simpler at home, and if you want to preserve some of the natural resources. You could also use one if you want to lean towards a healthier lifestyle as cooking in the crockpot is conducive to health than in the oven.

The crockpot can be used in making homemade and custom-made buffets, even in catering services. You can use it for cooking for your staff for special occasions and for showing them how to cook a tasty and healthier dish for your guests well within their own crockpot.

After choosing the best one for you, maybe it is time for you to know more about the recipes you should use. There are various recipes in this cookbook that are perfect for crockpot cooking, and they will definitely be useful and beneficial for you.

Moreover, whether you are a newbie or an experienced cook, you are going to love this cookbook as it is packed with every conceivable taste. You have discovered more than 1000 recipes in this cookbook that you can put into practice using your crockpot. You can always customize the recipes to suit your taste buds, as you can make any recipe mild or hot, sweet or sour; you have all the freedom to make the recipes your own. The best thing about cooking using a crockpot is that you just need to add the main ingredients, and no other complicated cooking preparation is needed; the crockpot will add most of the other ingredients for you.

signature twist on these recipes and let these recipes add magic to your life.

CPSIA information can be obtained
at www.ICGtesting.com
Printed in the USA
BVHW092250260421
605885BV00002B/88